PHILIP JAMIESON

SAUSAGES AND MASH

SHORT PLAYS FOR PAIRS AND GROUPS

Introduction

'Lies are man's most universal weakness, a recreation, a solace, a refuge (Mark Twain).'

These sketches are designed to be performed with the minimum of props and costumes and without the need for sets of any kind. The first few lines, in most cases, generally establish the setting for each play. Otherwise, a sentence or two can serve as an introduction. Props and stage directions are kept to a minimum, helping the directors shape their own fresh interpretations.

There are 19 sketches with a total cast of 52 and all are speaking roles. 12 are specifically female roles and 10 are male. The other 30 can be played by either gender. Characters intended to be male or female are identified at the start of the scripts.

The total performance time for this collection would be approximately 60 minutes.

Phil Jamieson

Contents

Pairs 1   Granny

Two men in their fifties are sat at a pub table

John   Phil. Remember when Granny told us about how she would go on those amazing picnics with her sisters when she was a little girl?

Phil   Yeah.

John   They'd take home- grown apples, egg sandwiches and Ribena to drink.

Phil   Yes. What's your point, brother?

John   Well, granny was a liar.

Phil   What?

John   Ribena was first produced in 1938. She would have been in her late forties when it was introduced.

       Pause

Phil   So, it wasn't around when she was a little girl?

John   I checked it out. So, if she lied about that, she could have lied about everything she told us, her beloved grandchildren.

Phil   Gosh. I see what you mean. All those anecdotes from her childhood, back in early 20th century might have been fake?

John   Just designed to enchant us, regardless of truth. I mean, did she really drive an ambulance in the 'great war'? I don't think so. Was her brother Eric actually a pilot? Was he really shot down over No-man's-land and captured by the Germans, held for six weeks?

Phil   Crikey! Was there really an Eric for that matter?

John   Yes. That photograph of him in his uniform, smoking a pipe could have been a photo of anybody. Can we really believe anything she said to us?

Phil   She was cruel as well. Remember when I was four and I got that stone stuck in the underside of my big toe?

John   Yes. I think so.

Phil   I had been warned not to play out in the back yard by granny and Mum. Well, Granny told me that if I didn't get it out soon, it would slowly work its way to my heart and kill me.

John   She actually said that?

Phil   I was mortified. I cried so much, convinced that I would croak it and never see any of you again.

John   Not surprising.

Phil   That was another big fat lie, wasn't it? Dad just picked the stone out with a pair of tweezers and I was good to go. That was about fifty years ago and that infantile fear and panic are still with me.

John   When you think about it, she was a massive fibber, a Victorian purveyor of porky pies. Remember though. One thing she never lied to me about. I never remember her telling me that she loved me. Can you remember her saying anything like that?

Phil   No.

John   That might have been one lie she could never bring herself to tell us?

Pause

What did she leave you when she died?

Phil shrugs

Nada! Nothing! Not a bean. Same with me. She must have had a ton of money somewhere. Granddad was

5

high up in an oil company. They had a big house in Preston and only three kids. Sally married a rich bloke and Kitty was a nun. So where did the money go?

Phil looks sheepish. Sudden realisation for John

What? Really? How much?

Phil   £500 in bonds.

John   She left you £500 in bonds.

Phil   Yeah. I thought you'd got the same. I was only ten when she died. You were thirteen. Mum and Dad put it in an account for me.

John   I didn't know anything about that. What about our little sister?

Phil   Suzie got the same.

John   Wow!

Pause

£500 in bonds. If you just left it in an account, you'd have a bundle by now.

Phil   I don't know what to say, John. I'm sorry.

John   It's not your fault, Phil. I bet she kept those bonds hidden away from Mum and Dad. She was really tight. HA! Another lie. Dad bought the house in the mid-fifties for about two thousand quid and Granny lived with the family rent free all those years.

Phil   Dad supported the lot of us on one wage. It must have been tough.

Pause

John   Don't get me wrong. I know I'm doing OK. I don't want her money, but I could have really used £500 when I was starting off in life.

Phil   Sorry.

John   You know, I don't think she even liked Ribena. I can never remember her drinking it.

Phil   She only drank tea.

Pause

John   And gin.

Phil   Oh yes.

Pairs 2   *Believe It Or Not*

A customer enters a book shop

A   Can I help you?

B   Yes. I'm looking for a book about ghosts.

A   We've got several titles to choose from. There's 'The A to Z of Ghosts', 'The Supernatural World', 'Ghost-finder' and 'Photographing Ghosts'.

B   I'll take them all.

A   Are you researching a book?

B   No. I think my house is haunted.

A   Really!

B   Yes, I've noticed some very strange things going on recently.

A   What sort of things?

B   Well, the other day I heard a strange noise coming from the loft. It was a sort of banging noise and then there's the lights.

A   What happens with the lights?

B   They flicker sometimes.

A   Oh! Have you been up to the loft to check?

B	Yes. I was terrified but I decided that I had to know what it was. I took a torch and went up there yesterday. What I saw made me decide to get some books on the subject.
A	What did you see?
B	It was a sort of glowing figure, leaning against the water tank.
A	What sort of figure? A person?
B	Yes, I think so. It was looking straight at me. Just staring.
A	That must have been terrifying. Was it a man or a woman?
B	It's hard to say. It was dressed in rags, dirty rags.
A	What did you do?
B	I just froze. It was looking right at me. Then it pointed at the water tank. Then it spoke to me.
A	What did it say?
B	"Look in here." That's all it said.
A	Well, did you look?
B	Would you?

A	I'm not sure. Not straight away. I'd have to think about it. What did you do?
B	I passed out.
A	What?
B	I fainted. I woke up about ten minutes later stretched out on my back in the loft. I was alone and it was pitch dark. It was very quiet too. Not the normal sort of quiet though. It's almost as if, when this thing disappeared, it had taken my senses with it.
A	What did you do next?
B	I got out of the loft quickly and made myself a cup of tea. I was very confused. I sat in the kitchen trying to gather my thoughts. Then about eleven at night I heard this tapping noise coming from the water pipes.
A	You must have been petrified.
B	Absolutely. The tapping grew louder. I felt like getting out, but it was almost hypnotic. I couldn't help myself listening.
A	Couldn't that have been trapped air or something?

Pause.

B	No, it was too regular. Like a rhythm. Three long taps followed by two short taps then two long taps (B demonstrates by tapping on the table).
A	Morse code! That sounds like a Morse coded message.
B	I wrote it all down. (Taking a piece of paper from his pocket and giving it to A) I've written every long tap as a capital T and each short one as a small T. There's three pages of it here.
A	Wait! I've got a book on Morse code somewhere. We can work out what it says. I won't be a moment.

A exits. B looks to see that no-one is watching then picks up the cash register and exits quickly. After a few seconds A returns reading aloud from a book.

A	I've worked out the code. It says 'Don't believe everything you hear'. (Looks up and sees there is nobody there) Where's he gone?

Pairs 3　　*There's Nothing To It*

A customer in a restaurant is approached by a waiter or waitress.

A　　　　　Are you ready to order?

B　　　　　What's the soup of the day?

A　　　　　It's water chestnut. It's the chef's speciality.

B　　　　　Water chestnut soup? What are the ingredients?

A　　　　　I'm not sure really. Shall I ask?

B　　　　　No, never mind. Do you have any veal?

A　　　　　Have you looked in the vegetarian section of the menu?

B　　　　　Veal is a kind of meat. Anyway, I haven't got a menu. You didn't bring me one.

A　　　　　I'm sorry. You see I'm new to the job.

B　　　　　I never would have guessed.

A　　　　　Yes. I only started this afternoon.

B　　　　　Well, you bring me the menu and I'll point to the things I want to order for my lunch.

A　　　　　Great! Thanks. I'll just go and get one.

A exits and returns with a menu.

A	Here you are. Enjoy your meal.
B	Thank you but you're meant to say that when you've brought the food.
A	But you haven't ordered any.
B	That's because you've only just brought me the menu.
A	I haven't really got the hang of it yet. Sorry.
B	Look. You sit here and I'll be the waiter. You order something and I'll demonstrate what you are meant to do. There's nothing to it.

They swap places.

A	(Looking at menu) Waiter! Can you bring me a menu please?
B	You are holding a menu in your hands.
A	This (He waves it in the air) is a wine list. I cannot order food from a wine list can I?

B exits then returns with a menu.

B	Here we are. May I recommend the chef's Special Mixed Grill.
A	No you may not. (Gives the menu straight back) I want egg and chips.

B	What?
A	I said I want egg and chips. Are you deaf or stupid?
B	You can't speak to me like that. I'm a customer.
A	No! I'm the customer and the customer is always right.
B	Look, we're only pretending. You're meant to look at the menu and choose something to eat. Then I take your order.
A	(Angry) Do you want me to get the manager in here?
B	No, of course not.
A	Then just get me the food I ordered.
B	But ...
A	GET ME MY MEAL NOW!
B	Sorry ... yes. I'm going.

B exits.

A	She's right you know. There's nothing to it.

Pairs 4   Nothing Magical?

Two friends in the countryside.

A   What a beautiful sun. It's like a big red ball. It looks like it's melting into the sea.

B   If you say so.

A   Wonderful.

B   It's not that wonderful really. The sun is just a big ball of gas burning in space. There are millions of suns out there. Some big, some bigger. There's nothing magical about them.

A   Listen!

B   Listen to what?

A   Total silence.

B   Then how can I listen?

A   You can feel it. That special silence just before sunset. It fills the earth with restful calm thoughts.

B   It fills me with boredom.

A   Don't you feel an inner peace?

B   I just feel tired and cold.

A	All the birds and animals are tucked up in their beds.
B	Lucky them.
A	The wind has dropped to a gentle breeze. The earth is at rest.
B	That's nonsense. It's just going dark.
A	Why do you think children are afraid of the dark?
B	I wasn't. Only superstitious idiots believe in monsters and ghosts and things that go bump in the night. Parents fill their children's heads with all that rubbish so they can control them.
A	What do you mean?
B	Little children will believe anything. Parents tell them that if they don't behave, the Bogey man will come and get them in the night.
A	But that's cruel. My parents never told me that.
B	Well, you were lucky. What about Father Christmas?
A	What about Father Christmas?

B	I bet they told you that if you were a good little child, Santa would bring you your special present.
A	Yes, they did. That wasn't meant to frighten me.
B	Wasn't it? I bet you really behaved well, hoping that Santa would bring you the gift you wanted. I bet you were frightened in case he didn't come.

A is silent.

B	You see. It's the same thing as the Bogey man. People just make things up to control other people, to control stupid little children.
A	I wasn't stupid. I was top of my class every term.
B	I'm not saying you were stupid. You just believe things because you want to believe them. Not because they're true.

Pause.

A	I feel a bit cold now. Let's go inside.
B	Good idea.
A	Can't see anything anymore.
B	It's too dark.

A   That doesn't mean there's nothing out there
           though.

B   What?

A   Just because you can't see something, doesn't
           mean it's not there.

They exit

Pairs 5   *Sandwich*

A   Do you want a sandwich?

B   What's in it?

A   Cheese.

B   Just cheese?

A   Cheddar cheese. Nothing else.

B   Are you sure?

A   Of course I'm sure. I made them myself.

B   Butter or margarine?

A   Butter.

B   Is it salted?

A   Do you mean the butter or the bread?

B   The cheese. Is it salted?

A   No. It's salt free. Look, do you want it or not?

B   (Taking the sandwich and looking at it closely) Is it vegetarian cheese?

A   (Impatiently) Which do you prefer? Vegetarian or non-vegetarian?

B   Vegetarian.

A	It's vegetarian cheese. Are you going to eat it or not?
B	No.
A	Why not?
B	I'm not hungry.

Pairs 6   *Foibles*

Railway station platform. B is seated on a bench. A approaches the bench.

A   Fancy meeting you here.

B   Oh, hello.

A   It's been a while hasn't it?

B   How are you?

A   As well as can be expected I suppose.

B   I see.

A   Oh, do you?

B   Look, that was a long time ago. We were different people then.

           Pause.

A   Do you mind if I sit down?

B   It's a free country.

           Pause. A sits.

A   Sorry.

B   What for?

A   For disturbing you.

B	You're not disturbing me. Why do you have to apologise all the time? That was one of the things that always got on my nerves about you. You were always apologising.
A	Yes, I suppose you're right. I'm sorry.
B	There you go again.
A	Alright, you've made your point. You weren't perfect yourself you know. You had your foibles.
B	And what's that meant to mean? What 'foibles'?
A	Well, there were plenty of things about you that used to annoy the hell out of me.
B	Such as?
	Pause.
A	Well, remember how you used to answer every question with another question?
B	What do you mean?
A	See? You just did it again, didn't you?
B	I just did what again?
A	You can't help it can you?
	Pause.
B	Who uses the word foibles anyway?

A   I've upset you now. I'm sorry. We were as bad as each other when I think about it. We'd go to the pub every Friday, have three pints, eat crisps and prattle on about 'them'. Do you remember 'them'?

B   Yes.

They exchange looks. Both smile.

A   They were the people that had an advantage. The folk that we blamed for our failings. THEM! They got rich or famous through nepotism or other folk's rubbish taste in music or acting. We never had the breaks they had. They had so many unfair advantages. **They** were in the right place at the right time. **They** were useful excuses for our own feelings of inadequacy.

B   Yeah! You've got a point there. We knew that our standards were higher than everyone else's. We had proper aspirations. We had taste and talent in bundles, but **they** got the breaks – 'them'. Of course, we never actually got up and did anything creative ourselves. I suppose we couldn't help the way we were, could we?

A	The way we are you mean? We're both oversensitive. The difference now is that we can both recognise it. It's not a weakness, being touchy. It's only a problem if you don't see it in yourself.
B	When did you become so philosophical? Look, let's keep in touch shall we?
A	Yes. Let's do that.
B	I don't know how to.
A	Good. That means I won't have to read your mindless babble anymore.
B	Charming.
A	I was only joking. Here's my card. Give me a call sometime. I've got to go now. I've got a train to catch.
B	(looking at watch) So have I and I better get a move on or I'll miss it.
A	Which train are you getting?
B	The six-thirty to Twickenham. How about you?
A	I'm going to Windsor. I better go. See you sometime.

A exits.

B sits alone on stage, looks at the card for a few seconds, smiles then slowly and deliberately tears it into little pieces. B then exits.

Pairs 7   Report

Two siblings.

A   What are you reading?

B   A letter.

A   Who's it from?

B   It's from school.

A   (Taking the letter from B) This is a report. You shouldn't have opened it.

B   (Snatching it back and reading aloud) F for Maths, F for English, G for Science, F for Art.

A   Mum and Dad will go mad. You shouldn't have opened it. The envelope was addressed to them. You're always doing stupid things.

B   We've got to get rid of it.

A   We can't do that.

B   Why not? They'll never know.

A   Honesty is the best policy. You've got to face up to this.

B   I'm going to burn it.

A   They'll ground you for a year when they find out.

B   They'll ground you for ten years if they read it.

A   What are you talking about?

B   (Hands the report to A) It's your report.

           Pause.

A   You get the matches. I'll get the ashtray.

Pairs 8   Birthday

A	Happy birthday. Here's your present.
B	Thanks. You shouldn't have bothered.
A	It's a surprise.
B	Great. I love surprises. It's beautifully wrapped.
A	The lady in the shop wrapped it for me. I bet you can't guess what it is.
B	I haven't got a clue.
A	Neither have I.
B	(Starting to unwrap it) What?
A	I can't wait to find out what it is.
B	But you bought it for me. You must know what it is.
A	I don't know. I asked the lady in the shop to choose something and wrap it up. I put my hands over my eyes like this while she was wrapping it up.
B	(Finishes unwrapping it) A pair of earrings. They're for pierced ears.
A	Brilliant! I never would have guessed that.

28

B	I don't wear earrings and anyway, even if I did, my ears aren't pierced.
A	They're your colour.
B	I don't wear earrings.
A	They match your eyes.
B	My eyes are brown and these are purple. Didn't you tell the lady anything about me?
A	No. I wanted it to be a total surprise. I just gave her a ten pound note and asked her to choose a gift and wrap it up.
B	Didn't you tell her how old I was or anything?
A	No, I wanted it to be a big ...
B	Surprise. I know. Well, thanks anyway.
A	I'm glad you like them.
B	I didn't say that.
A	Oh, I can exchange them for something else if you like.
B	You mean another total surprise?
A	I thought you'd be pleased.
B	I am. It's the thought that counts after all. It was very kind of you.

Pause.

It's your birthday next month isn't it?

A   Yes. On the fifteenth.

B   I can't wait.

Pairs 9   Rules

A female Head Teacher and a female pupil.

A   How many times have you been in my office,
           Jones?

B   I don't know, Miss Baker.

A   Do you want me to tell you?

Silence.

A   Too many! I'm tired of seeing you standing in
           front of this desk. Tired of hearing about your
           smoking and bullying in school. I'm sick of your
           bad language and vandalism. Don't you realise
           we have rules in this school?

B   Yes, Miss.

A   (Picks up a book from desk) There are thirty-six
           rules that govern behaviour in this school. You
           must have broken every one of them.

B   Not all of them.

A   What?

B   I've got as far as thirty-four.

A   (Looks in book) You mean that you have deliberately set out to break every rule in this book?

B   No. It was an accident.

A   What are you talking about?

B   Well, one day I just happened to look in the school handbook to see how many of the rules I had broken and I saw that I'd broken most of them.

A   You're proud of yourself aren't you? You're treating this like some sort of game.

B   (Moving towards the desk) It's not a game Miss. (B sits on the desk leans closer to A) It's my quest.

A   Get off this desk at once.

B   You see, I've only got to break one more rule and I've done the lot. All thirty-six stinking, stupid, pathetic rules.

A   You mean two more. You can't even count. You said you'd broken thirty-four, so that leaves two more rules. Perhaps if you'd paid more attention in Mathematics you would be able to understand that.

B   (Picking up the book and reading from it) Rule Thirty-Five says that 'Pupils must only sit down in the presence of the Head Teacher when told to do so.' (B drops the book on the floor) One more to go.

A   You think you're clever don't you? Well, you're a sad little loser Jones.

B   (Stands up quickly) What did you call me?

A   Loser.

B   You're not allowed to speak to me like that. I'm about to achieve something important and all you have to look forward to is retirement and sitting on your fat bottom for the rest of your miserable, boring life.

A   You'll achieve nothing Jones. Absolutely nothing.

B   I will be the only pupil ever to break every rule there is.

A   Not in this school. Now get out of my office.

B   (Quoting from the book) 'Any physical threat or assault on a member of staff will result in instant and permanent exclusion from the school.' (B moves close to A) You can't stop me now.

A   (Calmly picks up a sheet of paper from the desk and hands it to Jones). If you read this copy of a letter to your parents, providing you can read that is, you will see that you are formerly excluded from this school.

B   So?

A   Well, let me explain it simply so you can fully understand. This letter was sent in this morning's post. At the very moment it was posted, you were officially no longer a pupil in this school. Since you are no longer a pupil of the school, you cannot do anything that would break one of its rules.

B   You can't do that. You can't.

A   I have done it. I can however have you arrested if you like.

B   What are you talking about?

A   At this moment you are trespassing on School property.

B	You've ruined everything. I only had one more to break.
A	Can you please leave now?

B exits.

A	(Sighs deeply then speaks into the intercom on the desk) Mrs Blake. Could you make sure that letter to Mr and Mrs Jones goes in the next post.

Pairs 10   *Simpson*

An elderly gentleman and his butler.

A   Simpson!

B   (Entering) Yes, my lord.

A   You've been my butler for many years now.

B   Twenty years, my lord.

A   Twenty years is it? Well, in that time you have
           served my family very well. Very well indeed.

B   Thank you, my lord.

A   And I want you to know I have always valued
           your discretion and loyalty. You have been more
           than a servant. We consider you a friend.

B   That is very kind of you, sir.

A   There is a matter that I would like to talk to you
           about. It concerns your future.

B   My future, sir?

A   Have you given any thought to your golden years,
           Simpson?

B   My golden years, sir?

A   I mean retirement. You can't go on butlering
           forever you know.

B	I hadn't given it much thought, my lord.
A	Well I have. You're not a young man any more, Simpson. It's getting close to the time when a comfortable chair, a good book and Radio 4 beckon you.
B	Radio 4, my lord?
A	Comfort, Simpson. I'm talking about a comfortable retirement. Goodness knows you deserve it. Slippers, cup of cocoa and the occasional brandy. That sort of thing. No more stairs.
B	Well, I am getting very tired recently, my lord. Not that I'm complaining about the job. It's always been a pleasure serving the family.
A	I'll get right to the point. I don't see any good in beating around the bush. As you know, since I became a widower nearly ten years ago, Jonathan has been nothing but trouble. Quite frankly Simpson, he's been a bit of a pain in the neck. I know he's my only child but he's made it very clear that he doesn't want anything to do with the house or the estate.

B	He has certainly been a handful, my lord. I say that with the greatest of respect, my lord.
A	And now there's this.

He hands a letter to Simpson.

A	As you can see it's from North Africa. Jonathan has joined the French Foreign Legion. Read it would you Simpson.
B	'Dear Father, I have decided never to return home. I know this will come as no great surprise but ever since mother passed away, I've begun to despise the whole idea of all this wealth and property. Inside me is a simple man who wants only adventure. I don't want to inherit all that and end up as a crusty old lord in a crusty old house. Goodbye, Jonathan.'
A	So you can see what I'm trying to say Simpson, can't you?
B	Not really, my lord.
A	I'm going to leave it all to you old chap.
B	But ...
A	The house, the land, the rents, the farm. Everything.

B	My lord. Your son is still a young man. He might change his mind.
A	My mind is made up old friend. I'm nearly eighty-five now and you're only sixty-five. You'll have plenty of time to enjoy your retirement. Who can say how your life might turn out? You could decide to spend some time abroad, or just playing golf and enjoying yourself? It's up to you really. What about marriage? It's never too late to meet that special woman. I did. I was lucky. Why shouldn't you be?
B	I don't know what to say, my lord.
A	You don't have to say anything. Now, fetch me a brandy will you? There's a good chap. I'm not dead yet you know.
B	The Napoleon, my lord?
A	Of course. I'm determined to leave you not one drop of the Napoleon brandy. Not one drop.
B	Yes, my lord.

Simpson exits.

Pairs 11   Photographs

Two friends are indoors on a rainy day.

A   Now this is a picture of me on holiday in Brighton
            when I was five. Look, you can see the donkey in
            the background and I'm eating a Cornetto. Now
            this next one was taken in our old house. That's
            Rover the dog. She was only a puppy then.

B   She?

A   Yes, we thought Rover was a boy but she turned
            out to be a girl. Well, a bitch really. This one is
            funny. Do you know who that is buried in the
            sand?

B   (Sighs) No.

A   Go on. Have a guess.

B   I don't know who it is.

A   Go on. You'll kick yourself when I tell you.

B   Then why don't you tell me?

A   It's my cousin Helen. She was on holiday with us
            in Jersey.

B   But I've never met your cousin Helen. How could
            I guess?

A	Oh. I'll find you a photo of her.
B	If you must.
A	(Searching through the photographs) There must be one here.
B	It doesn't matter.
A	Here she is.
B	She's a little baby. You buried a little baby in the sand?
A	No, that was taken when she was three months old. She was much older on the other photo. Now, this is one of our old car. Can you tell what sort of car it was?
B	(Looks at photograph) It's a Volkswagen.
A	Wrong! It was a Golf. We used to love that old car.
B	A Golf is a type of Volkswagen.
A	I don't think so. My uncle's got a Golf and it doesn't look like that.
B	Your Uncle Bob has a Golf mark three. This is a Golf mark one. They look completely different but they're the same make of car.

A	Well, if you say so. Anyway, here's a picture of someone you'll recognise.
B	I'm sorry but I don't want to look at any more photographs. I'm a bit bored. Let's go outside. It's a beautiful day.
A	It's raining outside.
B	It was raining three hours ago when you suggested we came to your house and looked at some pictures. It's sunny now.
A	Well, I'm sorry I bored you.

Silence.

B	(Picks up the last photograph) This is me. I hardly recognised myself. I remember this being taken. I'd just got my Spiderman costume for my birthday. I wore it for days. You got a Batman outfit, with the Utility Belt and Baterang. This is great. Have you got any more?
A	I've got a whole box of them upstairs. Photos of you and me from years ago. Shall I get them?
B	Yes. Brilliant! I'll make some tea.

A exits. B looks at the photograph, smiles then exits.

Groups 1   *Sausages and Mash*

For four actors. A and B are male. C and D are female.

A   What are you playing, Daniel?

B   Megadestroyer.

A   Megadestroyer? You're just shooting at things.

B   They're aliens.

A   Yes, but why are you shooting at them?

B   They're trying to capture my base.

A   Oh.

             Pause.

A   Where is this base?

B   It's on the moon.

A   Why have you got a base on the moon?

B   I don't know. Oh, no!

A   What happened?

B   I've been destroyed. I've only got one life left now.

C   (Entering with a magazine) What's another word for Elk? It's five letters beginning with M and ending in E.

C sits in a chair at the table.

A	(Joining C at the table) Let me think.
B	Moose.
C	Yes, that fits. Thanks.
A	How can you do that? How can you concentrate on that game and think up the answer to a crossword clue at the same time?
B	I don't know. Got him!
A	Ask me another one.
C	O.K. A considered opinion or judgement. Nine letters. Blank S, blank I. Five blanks then an N.
A	Er, let's see.
B	Estimation.
A	(Standing) I can't believe it! He just sits there, shooting at aliens on the moon and gets all the answers.

C takes an iPod out and puts the earphones in.

A	What are you doing? I thought we were doing the crossword.
C	I'm just listening to Ricky Gervais. He's very funny.
B	Yes! Only two to go.

A	(Sits again) Ask me another one.
C	(Lifting one earphone) Pardon?
A	Ask me another clue. You're not to answer this Daniel. It's just for me.
C	(Puts earphone back over ear) To bungle. Four and two.
A	Have you got any of the letters?
C	What?
A	(Shouts) Any letters?
B	Foul up. What's for dinner Suze?
D (voice)	Sausages and mash.
A	What did you say?
B	Foul Up. That's the answer.

C laughs out loud at the downloaded comedy.

A	(Angry) I asked you not to answer this one. It was just for me.
B	Sorry, I wasn't listening.
A	(Frustrated) You must have been listening or you wouldn't have heard the clue.

C writes in another answer and laughs out loud again. D enters with some knitting, picks a book up from the table, sits cross legged on the floor, opens the book and lays it on the floor. D starts knitting and reading at the same time.

D   (Knitting and reading) Are you winning Daniel?

B   Nearly broken your scoring record. Only got one stage to go.

A just stares at D.

D   I met Colin today. He's much better now. He sends his regards.

C   Three letters. Porcine is the clue.

D   Pig. That's the answer. This book is great.

A   Can't anybody just concentrate on one thing at a time? Is it too much to ask?

D   Does anybody mind if I put the radio on? Chelsea are playing Man City.

A   That's it! I'm going out.

B   Beaten it. I've beaten the record. Yes!

D   Well done, Daniel.

A   If people would just concentrate on one thing at a time, we'd get a lot more done in this world.

Silence.

A   I'm going out.

A exits.

Groups 2   Fully Fitted

C is male and B is female. A can be either.

A   And this is the kitchen. It's fully fitted.

B   Lovely! It's so big! What do you think Phil?

C   It's a bit dark isn't it?

A   There's plenty of storage and this door connects with
       the dining room.

B   Brilliant! The whole family could sit down to lunch in
       here.

C   Oh, great. That'll be nice.

A   Shall we look upstairs now?

B   Yes. This place is so much bigger than I expected.

C   If you say so.

B   What's the matter Phil ?

A   I'll lead the way then.

A exits

B   What's the matter with you?

C   This isn't right

B   What's wrong with it?

C   It doesn't feel like home.

B   Look. You agreed that we should think about getting a house. The flat's too small. It's depressing. This is a nice area, Phil. We should give it a chance.

Pause

Oh, I get it. It's Molly.

C   She was part of us, remember? She was part of the place. If we leave there, we leave her behind. As long as we're in the flat, I feel like she's still with us. You must feel that as well, Suzie?

B   No! Actually, I don't feel that at all. Molly was a massive part of our lives, but she's gone, Phil, and there's nothing that'll bring her back.

C   I just...

B   I know, Phil. I can still love her, even from here.

C   I can't leave her behind. She's still there.

B   Look at this place. It's beautiful! It's massive! We can afford to do this, Phil. We can start a family here. There's enough space. The flat's too small. She's not coming back.

                      Pause

      It hurts me too. More than I thought possible.

C   Why did I leave the gate open? I always close it. Why?

B   Stop this now! Stop it, Phil. It wasn't your fault. It's a busy road and she was always trying to get out. She was an old dog and you know what we used to say.

C   You can't teach an old dog new tricks.

B   Yes. This place would be great for a couple of kids. What do you think?

A enters

A   Shall I just leave you to have a look around? I'll wait in the car.

C   No, it's fine. Lead the way.

A   Great. Let's have a look upstairs.

They exit

Groups 3   Welsh Gold

Three young women. They're in their early to mid- twenties.
They're well- heeled, country types.

A   Wow! Is that the ring?

B   Isn't it fantastic? There's six diamonds.

C   You're so lucky Lizzy.

A   He must be very rich.

B   We're very happy. That's Welsh gold. It's very rare.

C   Charlie and I have decided to leave it a while.

A   That's very sensible, Chloe.

B   We're going to The Cayman Islands for the Honeymoon.

C   There's no point in rushing.

B   We've hired a Jamaican steel band for the reception.

A   Fantastic! Was that Greg's choice?

B   Yes. Why? Does that matter?

A   No. I was just asking because I know that he loves that sort
        of music.

B   Yes, well, I like that sort of music too. I said that he could choose the band.

A   Great. Gosh! Are you writing your own vows?

B   Kind of. Well, I'll let you both in on a little secret.

B and C lean in to listen

I'm actually writing his vows as well as mine. It's not really something you could trust a chap with, is it? I mean, his vows would be sort of jokey and a little bit embarrassing. He always lets me make these decisions.

C   That's a good idea. Guys can be a little insensitive. They're not good at, you know, expressing their true feelings.

A   Are you having a Roller?

B   We're having a gold and silver coach drawn by four horses from Mandy's stables.

A   Wow! That's brilliant! It's so romantic.

C   I love horses. They can be so loyal and dependable.

A   You have invited Mandy, haven't you?

B   Of course I have. I couldn't really use her horses without asking her to come, could I? Besides, how could I have a proper wedding without the Chief Bridesmaid?

A   Mandy's the Chief Bridesmaid?

B   Naturally.

A   Oh.

C You can trust a horse.

B Wait until you see the fabrics for the Bridesmaids' dresses. You're all going to look like Disney princesses. I'll just go and fetch the swatches. The apricot fabric is beautiful.

B exits

A Did you know about this?

C What?

A Mandy's the Chief Bridesmaid. Lizzy's hardly seen Mandy since they left Uni. It just seems odd that she should ask her. Don't you think so, Chloe?

Pause

Chloe! Are you listening?

C Charlie's not going to the wedding.

A What? Why?

C When I told him about it, he said that he hates weddings and funerals and has no desire to attend either sort of event.

A He might change his mind. You should speak to him.

C That wouldn't make any difference.

A Do you want me to say something?

C No. It doesn't matter. Thanks. Are you still teaching?

A No. It was tough, you know, and besides, Mummy said I could work for her at the publishers any time I fancied.

Anyway, I was only training, so it's not as if I was leaving them high and dry or anything.

C   Oh.

A   To tell you the truth, I didn't really like the kids. They got on my wick a bit. You know, I'm not sure I get on with other people's sprogs at the best of times. I'm OK with my little sister, but she's family, you see. This class, 5F, really took the biscuit though. They set out, right from the start, to wind me up. It was jolly difficult to keep my cool with them.

So, one Monday, I got my own back. We were supposed to be having 'Reading Time'. That's when they sit quietly and listen to a story. I was trying to read them 'The Fish that Wished', but they were constantly interrupting, making silly noises and just mucking about. Anyway, I stopped reading and asked them if anyone had ever had a pet goldfish. Loads of little hands shot up immediately. Great! I then told them how common swim bladder infections are in goldfish and how they make the poor fish just float on the surface of the water looking as if they are dead. I then explained how, every year, lots and lots of pet fish are buried, flushed down the toilet, or just thrown away with the rubbish because their owners think they've just copped it. Well, the classroom went deathly quiet for about five seconds, and then it started. Eyes widened in horror and the sobbing started. It was wonderful. I thought only one or two would break down, but I was wide of the mark. First Poppy, then Camilla, both Sophies, and even the wickedest little troll of them all, Celina. It was fabulous. I'd won.

B returns carrying some swatches of fabric

B   You'll faint when you see this stuff. Doesn't this crimson go superbly with the Apricot Blush? I wouldn't have though they'd match, but they seem to.

A   You're right. You wouldn't expect them to go together so well. What do you think, Chloe?

C   That's often the way with things. Some things go together and some don't, even if you'd like them to.

                    Pause

B   This is so exciting. Let's go and get some wine and we can talk some more about the wedding. I can show you the invitations and the favours.

A and B exit

C   I'd like to thank the happy couple for giving me the opportunity to say a few words. I know it's usually only the Best Man, Father of the Bride and the Groom that get to say heart-warming and cheeky, embarrassing things about these two, but I'm honoured. I really am. I've known Lizzy since secondary school and she's always been a great friend. She was the one that taught me how to plait my hair. She showed me how to put make-up on in a manner that didn't make me look like Crusty the Clown and boosted my confidence when it was pretty low. It was Lizzy who eventually introduced me to Charlie when we were in Upper Sixth. It felt great to actually have a boyfriend, instead of always being the third wheel. It meant that I could be asked to go to parties and things as part of a legitimate couple and not simply out of sympathy. I felt really good about myself. Now, ironically, four short years later, it's Charlie who's brought me to my lowest ebb, my complete and utter lack of all self-belief.

> Pause

Look. Sorry. This isn't about me. It's about Lizzy and Greg. It's their day. (She raises an invisible Champagne flute) Lizzy and Greg!

D enters

D   Hello Chloe.

C   Hi Mandy. Are you looking for Lizzy?

D   Yes. Is she about?

C   She's just popped inside with Abby. They're looking at wedding stuff.

D   I've come straight from the stables, so I'm a bit of a mess (Indicates her clothes). Would you tell her something for me?

C   Of course. What is it?

D   Look, to be honest, I'm a bit of a coward when it comes to letting people down. You see, her wedding's the same week as Badminton and daddy definitely wants me there. We've got three horses taking part anyway and it's sort of a family tradition.

C   Do you want me to tell her all of this? Wouldn't it be better to send Lizzy an email or a letter?

D   I think it'd be better if you told her. I just said yes straight away. I was really flattered that she'd asked me. I mean, we hadn't spoken much since we graduated.

C   No problem. I'll tell her when you've gone. Nice to see you again, Mandy. Good luck at Badminton.

D   Cheers! That's brilliant. Thanks.

D exits. A and B enter

B   Was that Mandy? Did she want to see me?

C   It's not great news, I'm afraid, Lizzy.

A   Oh, gosh. What?

B   What?

C   Badminton is on at the same time as the wedding and she has to go there.

B   She can't be Chief Bridesmaid?

C   No. I'm afraid not.

A   What a shame.

B   Oh, no!

A   What is it?

B	The horses! Are they taking all the horses? We need the horses for the carriage.
C	I don't know. Mandy said they're taking three horses.
A	Well, you can't have one horse pulling the carriage. It'd look silly.
B	Everything's falling apart. What am I going to do?
A	'Phone her! Ask her if you can still have the horses.
B	I can't do that. I'd sound desperate and needy.

Pause

Quick! Run after her, Abby. Ask her for me. You know the way to the stables.

A exits at speed

I can't ask her myself. You can see that can't you, Chloe?

C	Of course.
B	Chloe. Could I ask you a massive favour?
C	Depends on what it might be. Go on.
B	Would you be my Chief Bridesmaid?
C	Really?
B	Of course. I'll let you in on a little secret. I only really asked Mandy for the use of the horses. I've hardly seen her since Uni. And we didn't really hang out much there. I should have asked you in the first place. Sorry.

C   What about Abby?

B   She'll understand. She'll be fine.

C   I'm flattered. Why me though?

B   You're calmer than Abby. You just take things in your stride. That's the great thing about you. Say yes.

Pause

C   I'll do it on one condition.

B   What?

C   You ditch the apricot fabric. It's vile.

B   (Laughs) Agreed! What was I thinking?

C and D exit

Groups 4   *Norris and Florris*

B is male. C and D are female. A can be played by either male or female.

A and B on one side of the stage/C and D on the other side of the stage.

A   This is the fifth time you've been sent to my office Norris.

C   Congratulations Florris!

B   So what?

D   Thank you Miss Smith.

A   I'll tell you what! I'm going to telephone your parents today.

C   Your parents will be so proud. We're giving you a special prize.

B   I don't care.

D   Oh goody!

A   Why can't you be more like your sister?

C   Why can't your brother be more like you?

B   Are we finished here?

D   He just won't listen to anyone, Miss Smith.

A   Well, one of us is finished, Norris. I'm excluding you from school.

C   Will you speak to him? He might listen to you?

B   Can I go now? I'm bored.

D   I'll do my best. Thank you Miss Smith. Goodbye.

B and D exit and meet at Down Stage Centre

D   Hello Norris.

B   Right sis!

D   Are you in trouble again?

B   Potter's excluded me.

D   Not again!?

B   I think it's for good this time.

D   What did you do?

B   We glued some of the lockers shut.

D   What? Wait a minute. We? Who else did this?

B   Charlie and Lewis.

D   You're taking the blame for them again?

B   They're my mates. They'd do the same for me, wouldn't they?

D   Have they? You're the only one being excluded.

B   You don't get it do you?

D   What? What don't I get?

B   Loyalty. I'm not just in it for me.

D   Look! They're laughing at you. They've got away with it. You haven't.

B   Can you tell mum and dad for me?

D   Why can't you tell them?

B   I don't know. I just can't.

D   Alright. I'll break it to them gently by telling them the good news first.

B   Thanks sis. What good news?

D   I'm getting another award.

B   Yeah, that's great. What's it for this time?

D   Creative Writing. I should get one for Diplomacy.

B   (shouting) Hoy! Charlie! Lewis! Wait!

D   Norris. Don't go after them. They're nothing but trouble.

B   Yeah. That's what I want. Trouble. Nothing but trouble.

D   Yes. That's the trouble. Fast-forward fifteen years.

B exits. D lingers for a few seconds then exits also. Table is positioned CS, narrow edge facing the audience and a chair at either long edge. B enters and, after a deep sigh, sits on one of the chairs. D enters, scowls at him and then sits in the other chair.

D   So?

B   It's good to see you sis.

D   Is it? Really! We're sitting in a prison visiting room. The circumstances could be better.

B   How are you anyway?

D   As well as can be expected.

B   Mum and dad send their love. Mum said they'll try to get here on Wednesday.

D   Tell her not to bother.

B   Don't be like that, Flo.

D   She's been in twice already and I've only been here for a week. And (hushed voice) don't call me Flo. I call myself Frankie in here. It's less…you know…little girly than Flo. You've got to maintain a tougher exterior in places like this. Frankie sounds more streetwise. You should see some of the girls in my wing. There's tattoos and nose rings all over the place.

B   It's not exactly high security in here though is it? I mean, you're doing six months for fiddling the books.

You're not exactly on Scotland Yard's most wanted list.

D   I did not fiddle any accounts. There were some avoidable errors and, as Chief Accountant, I took full responsibility.

B   You took a little more than that though, didn't you? A quarter of a million pounds wasn't it?

D   Alright. The money has been recovered, nobody's dead nor injured and…here I am. How is the window cleaning job going?

B   Good. There's a lot of dirty windows in Aintree. I'm cleaning up.

D   Ha. Very witty.

B   Windows can be a bit of a pain though.

D   Enough! Save some of the rubbish jokes for next time.

B   Charlie was asking about you.

D   Oh?

B   He wanted to know when you're coming out. I think he fancies you.

D   What? Now that I'm a hardened criminal you mean? Now that I'm a bit dangerous to know. He's never really spoken to me, let alone chatted me up. Like the rest of your friends, he actively avoided teachers' pets like me at school. What about Lewis? He only got friendly with me when I passed my driving test. He only wanted a lift to the pub. Forget it! I wouldn't be seen dead with Charlie.

B   Still too good for my mates then? Even in here?

D   Thanks for that.

B   It was only a joke. I'm sorry Flo.

D   Frankie! It's Frankie in here.

B   I'm sorry, Frankie.

D   Wow. If anybody ever wanted a practical example of irony, they'd only have to witness this moment with you and me.

B   What do you mean?

D   Come on! Think about it. What you were like at school. I was the sensible one. Ha!

B   Hey! Why don't we swap places? After all, we are twins. We look a bit alike.

D   Idiot!

B   It'd do you some good to get out and I'm going stir crazy living with Mum and Dad. I could bring a wig next time and pad myself out a bit. Here and there

D   (smiling) Oh, sure. That'd really suit you wouldn't it? A few months in a 'Girls Only' wing. You'd have a captive audience.

B   Nice.

D   They wouldn't be able to tell you to get lost or beat it, like all the other girls do. You can't do either of those things in here. They'd be stuck with you.

B   Look. When you get out, why don't we go abroad? Spain?

D   And do what?

B   Go into business together!

D   Doing what?

B   Landscape Gardening? Window Cleaning? Fiddling Accounts? I don't know.

D   Are you mad?

B   Why?

D   Look. You'd have to be crazy to go into business with someone who has served a prison sentence for fraud.

B   How would anyone know?

D   Norris! This is the modern world. The minute you're found guilty of anything, that information is circulated around every EU state. I will be the most unwelcome of guests anywhere in Europe.

B   What about America?

D   What? I wouldn't stand a chance of getting my foot through that particular door. They've got pretty high standards and they don't look too kindly upon fraudsters, regardless of the magnitude of their crime.

B   You could change your name?

D We look alike, Norris! Folk are going to put two and two together and work out that I'm your sister.

B You're getting paranoid.

D No. I'm trying to put you off. I'm nothing but trouble. You'd be better off disassociating with me.

B Disa....what?

D Pretending that you don't know me. Saying that you don't have a sister.

B No! No chance! Were in this together.

D What? In what together? What are you talking about? There's no 'this'.

B I'll cover for you. Like you did for me. When we were children. You explained things to Mum and Dad. You made them understand.

D I lied, Norris. I lied to them. To get you off the hook.

B I'll lie for you.

D No! Go home.

B   I will.

D   You won't! I won't let you. Go home. Look after
         yourself. Look after mum and dad. Come and see me
         soon. You know where to find me. I'm not going
         anywhere, after all.

They hug. B exits and D stands, shrugs, turns up collar and
adopts a tough pose.

         The name's Frankie. Who are you looking at?

D exits.

Groups 5   No Mirrors

Two guests are shown into their hotel room.

A   This is your room.

B   It's very spacious.

C   Excellent view. You can see the castle and the river.

A   Yes. Breakfast is served at 8am. Dinner can be taken
       on the terrace.

B   Is there room service?

A   Yes. Just pick up that phone and dial 9. Someone will
       answer.

C   Good. I'm starving.

A   There are some rules.

B   Oh.

A   No pets are allowed in the rooms.

C   Yes, naturally.

A   No garlic allowed in here. Customers must close all the curtains if they leave the room during the day.

B   Really?

A   For the safety of our maids.

C   Seriously?

A   Yes.

B   Of course. That's no problem. Thank you.

A   I have to leave now. Here are your keys. Enjoy your stay.

A exits

C   That was unusual.

B   There are no mirrors in this room.

C   There must be one in the bathroom. I'll have a look.

C exits

B   This place is a bit creepy. It's all a bit old fashioned.

C   There's no mirror in here, Chris. This bathroom is massive!

(B exits. The following spoken from offstage)

B   Wow! It's bigger than the bedroom. What's that box thing?

C   It looks like a chest freezer. Why would they keep a fridge freezer in a bathroom?

B   It looks more like a tomb.

C   Yes. I'm going to have a peek inside.

B   Do you think we should?

C   Yeah. It can't do any harm.

B   Here goes.

(Blackout)

C   Hey! Who turned the lights off?

From offstage, there's a creaking sound followed by a prolonged scream

Sound of key in lock and A enters

74

A   Hello! Excuse me. Sorry for the intrusion, but I forgot
      to mention that there's a shared bathroom. Hello? Are
      you there?

C is male. A and B can be either male or female.

B   (Speaking on the telephone) I'm working late today Mother. Yes, I'll 'phone you before I leave here. I'm going to call in at Tesco's on the way home. I'll get your tea bags there. No. Don't try to alter the heating. Leave it until I get back. Last time you messed with it, it was like a Turkish bath. OK, well, put some more clothes on. There's a shawl on the back of one of the chairs in the Dining Room. I know. I understand. No, I don't know where your slippers are. Put another pair of socks on. I've got to go now. There's a customer. See you later Mum. Bye.

A   Good morning.

B   Good morning. How can I help you?

A   Well, I've brought this coat back. I collected it yesterday but when I got it home, I found this mark on it.

B   (Looking closely at the coat) Did you have the four star or the five star cleaning?

A   The five star cleaning.

B	Phil
C	(Entering) Yes?
B	Did you serve this customer?
C	Yes, I think so.
B	Do you have a receipt?
A	Here it is. Can you get the mark off?
B	(Looks closely at the receipt) I'm afraid not. This is a permanent stain. The five-star service does not guarantee the removal of permanent marks.
C	I think this is an oil stain. Probably motor oil.
A	This mark wasn't on the coat when I brought it in.
B	Are you sure?
A	Yes. It was perfect.
C	I'm sure I would have noticed a stain like this.
B	Would you Phil? Were there many people in here when you took this order?
C	There were quite a few. It was lunch time, but...
B	So you were very busy?
C	Well, yes.

B	(with a weak smile) And you're not getting any younger, are you Phil?
A	Excuse me. This coat did not have a stain on it when I brought it in. Your assistant has just confirmed that.
B	Not really. Phil was dealing with a lot of customers at the time. We can't expect an inexperienced member of staff to notice every detail when he's working under pressure.
C	I've worked here for fifteen years.
A	Are you suggesting that I'm lying?
B	Not at all. I'm simply saying it's possible that you didn't notice the mark when you brought the coat in for cleaning.
A	And it's possible that I didn't notice the mark because it wasn't there.
C	I wasn't really that busy.
B	Thank you, Phil. You can go and have your lunch break now.
C	I don't have my lunch until one.
B	You can have an early lunch.

A	This is ridiculous. Either you get rid of this mark or I get my money back.
B	I'm afraid we don't give refunds. It's a company policy.

C exits.

A	This is a rotten way to treat a customer. I want to speak to the manager.
B	Customer complaints are dealt with at our Head Office. Do you wish to make a complaint?
A	Yes, I do. This is terrible.
B	If you fill in one of these forms, I'll see that it gets to the Complaints Department.

A takes the form and fills it in.

A	I'd hardly worn this coat. There's no way that I could have got motor oil on it. I haven't even got a car. It's ruined. Completely ruined. Well, your company is going to pay for it. You can't treat people like this.

A completes the form, slams it down on the counter and begins to exit.

B	(Holding out the coat) Don't forget this.

A returns to the counter, grabs the coat and exits.

B reads the form, crumples it up into a ball and drops it onto the floor. C moves to DSC. He is carrying a lunch bag and fishes out a sandwich.

C   I hate lying. I really do. When my brother was in his twenties, he used to look in on an old lady who lived in the flat above his in Bristol. Florence was about ninety and pretty well blind and chair-bound. Well, she had a skinny little ancient cat that was also blind. Florence had owned Tabby since she was a tiny kitten. Three times a day, Tabby used to drag herself to her feet and stagger in a weary circle around the lounge, passing under Florence's outstretched hand. It wasn't much in the way of comfort for either of them, but it was enough. Somehow Florence always knew when the cat was heading towards her and sensed exactly when to poke out her bumpy little hand and brush the length of her beloved.

One afternoon, when my brother had dropped in to open a jar of jam for his elderly neighbour, Florence suddenly took ill and was whisked off to the local hospital. My brother had 'phoned for the ambulance himself and, being in possession of a spare key, was obliged to call in each day to feed Tabby. He also changed the litter and got into the habit of taking Florence's place in the armchair, hand outstretched, palm down for Tabby's regular stroke. The cat didn't seem to notice the difference.

A week later, Florence was back in her chair. It had merely been something to do with her dodgy blood pressure. Then the cat went and died. My brother discovered Tabby's little corpse when he went in to check on her owner. Like a good neighbour, he made some tea for Florence and then secretly went out and buried her in the communal gardens. He told the old lady that he was taking the bin bag out. Florence still extended the hand at the next cat moment. What was he to do? My brother had no choice other than to take grab the fake feather duster from a shelf and pass it gently under her palm. He held his breath. Florence didn't notice the difference. He kept this up for two weeks or so and then Florence herself died. It's tempting to tell you that it was from a stroke, but it wasn't. It was something else to do with her brain and being very old.

My brother didn't have to keep up the pretence any more. The people that taught him and me might say that that he shouldn't have deceived the old lady. As for the cat? I don't know if that counts as a lie? Is it only a sin to lie to a human being? Either way, according to a lot of people, he did wrong. The right thing would probably have been to take Florence by her little old hand and to have told her in a soft voice that Tabby had passed away and was in a better and more peaceful place. She was somewhere where she could run and catch mice again, a perfect garden in which it was always summer and milk and fish flowed freely.

My brother's name is Paul. I don't know why I didn't mention that before. Anyway, he's always been a head-on sort of person. You know. He would never just walk away from a challenge or some problem. His response will be direct and uncomplicated, or completely the opposite to that. You know, unnecessarily complex, like the whole cat thing.

Anyway, an example of one of his straightforward, no nonsense reactions happened about a month or so ago. Myself and my two kiddies were his passengers on the way to Sainsbury's one afternoon when he was cut up at a roundabout by an old silver Astra. Paul beeped his horn, more as a kind of natural reaction than through rage or anything. Neither of us mentioned it. It was just one of those things. Less than a minute after we'd parked at the store and were releasing the two children, the silver Astra glided into the space next to ours. He must have double-backed and followed us.

The first we knew of this was a bloke's voice, a strong Wiltshire accent informing us that it was a good thing we had two kids in the back or he would (expletive) kill us. I turned in surprise to see two guys, the speaker at the wheel. He was considerably younger than Paul and me, but, I couldn't help noticing, neither man had exited the car. We were being addressed through the open driver's window. His passenger looked to be in his mid-fifties and was silent. He just seemed to be staring, sizing me up.

I re-buckled the kids back into their car seats and wondered how this would play out? Paul walked straight toward the speaker and asked him how he intended to kill us? Did the driver have a gun or knife? Was he going to run us over? Were both the occupants intent on doing away with us, or would it be the driver acting alone? Don't get me wrong. Paul wasn't being a smart Alec or anything like that. He was just curious and, it seemed, not in the least concerned for his safety.

The confusion on the driver's face was tempered only by his indignation. He looked as if he was genuinely baffled by the question. How WOULD he carry out a double murder in broad daylight with many possible witnesses? And then the mood changed rapidly and, in my view, for the better. At that moment, the Astra's passenger leaned towards the open window and, with a confirmatory flash of recognition, hailed me.

'Phil! How the hell are you, old boy?

I instantly recognised Peter, an old friend from school. He introduced the driver as his son, Will.

We chatted and caught up for a few minutes. You can imagine how uncomfortable the driver felt and his expression oscillated between embarrassment and deep, deep regret. Paul returned to our car and re-released the impatient twosome. I couldn't help noticing the very slightest look of disappointment on his face. The Astra drove off with a friendly beep. Had Peter persuaded his driver that we were good chaps after all? Were we good chaps after all? I mean, we hadn't really taken the high ground here, had we?

I can't help thinking about Paul's look of regret. What was he hoping for there? A battle of wits? Probably not. He'd already won that hands down. Did he actually want the driver to explain his plan to do away with us? I don't know. We've never talked about the incident.

Groups 7* *Pointless*

For five actors. A is male and D is female. The other three can be either.

A   Don't jump. Think about what you're doing.

B   There's nothing left for me. It's pointless!

A   There's always a point to life.

B   I've lost my job. My relationship's ruined. Everything's a mess.

A   There must be something to live for. Be careful!

B   I'm going to jump. That's it.

A   But everybody has got something to live for.

B   What have you got that's so special?

A   Well.....there's.....erm.....erm.....this watch! My father left me this watch. It was given to him as a retirement gift.

B   Is that all?

A   Isn't that enough?

B   What time is it?

A	(Looks at watch) Six. No, that can't be right. It's stopped! I don't believe it.
B	Right. This is it. I'm going to jump now.
A	Wait! I'm going with you. Move over will you. You're right you know. There's no point to it really.
C	Stop! Just step back from the edge both of you. Remain calm.
B	We're going to jump, Officer. We've got no reason to go on.
C	I am a custodian of the law and I am ordering you to step back from the edge.
A	(Imitating C) A custodian of the law. You're just a copper. You can't order us to do anything.
C	Step back, or ...
B	Or what? You'll arrest us?
C	(Starts to cry) It's no good. I'll never be a proper Police Officer.
A	There's nothing to be ashamed of. Not everyone's cut out for it.

C	(Blubbering) You don't understand. It's all I ever wanted to be, since I was a child. I used to watch 'Law and Order' and dream of being a tough but honest Police Officer. Now I can't even talk you two down.
B	You can't expect to succeed every time.
C	(Sniffing) This is the last straw. I've only been training for three weeks and I've already failed every training exercise.
B	Look, I'm very sorry and all that but we're going to jump off this roof now.
C	I'm coming too.

All three join hands. One ... two ...

D	Wait!
B	What now? What do you want?
D	Don't jump!
A	Aren't you Miss Brown?
D	My surname is Brown, yes. Do I know you?
A	It's me, Chris Mills. I was in your Infants' class at St. Margaret's.

D	Oh, yes. That must have been over fifteen years ago. You've certainly grown up.
C	Can we cut the tearful reunion short and get on with the suicides.
E	(suddenly entering) What the hell is going on here?
B	Go away. We're busy.
D	Why are you doing this, Chris?
A	Well, I'm a complete failure. I've failed at everything. We've failed at everything we needed to succeed at. Jobs, relationships, schools.
E	Feet!
C	What did you say?
E	I couldn't get into the army because I had flat feet. It's all I ever wanted to do.
B	So that's why you're up here on the roof?
E	Yes. Make some room please.
D	I failed you didn't I?
A	What?

D	I let you down as a teacher. I didn't give you the start you needed in life. You needed a push to get you started on the right path and I failed you.
A	It wasn't your fault, Miss Brown.
D	I'm joining you.
C	For goodness sake, can we just get on with it?
D	On the count of three everybody.
All Five	One ... two ...

Groups 8   Bus

A arrives at a Bus Stop. B, C and D are waiting for a bus.

It's Liverpool. It's raining. It's the 1970's. It's wet and miserable.

A   How long have you been waiting here?

B   Oh, about half an hour. I think I just missed one.

C   There's meant to be one due in about ten minutes.

A   Thanks.

B   It's a reduced service tonight.

A   Pardon?

B   They're running a reduced service. You can usually guarantee one every fifteen minutes or so but not tonight.

D   It's always like this on New Year's Eve.

C   Always the same.

                    Pause.

D   And Christmas Eve.

B   It's worse on Christmas Eve. I waited hours on Christmas Eve.

A   Hours?

91

B	Well, a long time anyway.
D	I had to get a taxi last year. I waited two hours but it turns out I'd missed the last one. It went at ten thirty instead of eleven thirty.
B	Typical.
C	Yeah.
A	Have you seen any taxis around tonight?
D	I saw one earlier. It was full though.
B	They're very busy tonight.
A	I think I might walk up as far as Boots and see if I can get one.
C	It's a long walk.
B	If you start walking, you might miss the bus.
D	Then you'll have a longer walk. It's a bit of a risk.
A	Well, it's getting a bit cold and I might as well try.
B	But what if you don't find one?
A	There's a telephone box at the corner of Duke Street. I'll 'phone from there.

C	They don't take telephone bookings on New Year's Eve. You'll be much better off waiting here.
D	With us.

Pause.

B	It should be here any minute.
A	Well, I'm off!
C	No! Think about what you're doing. It's cold. It's probably going to rain.
D	Or snow.
C	You'll get wet and tired out. It's happened to me before.
B	And me, more than once.
A	Look. I'd better be going.
D	Wait! I can see it coming.
C	Yes, so can I.
A	I can't see it.
B	Where?
C	Just turning the corner by the statue. You can see it indicating.

A	I can't see anything. The road is empty. I'm going to get a taxi.

A starts to exit.

D	Don't!
A	What's the matter?
D	My heart!

D falls to the floor, clutching his chest. B and C run to him. A stands staring.

C	Help him. Somebody help him.
B	(To C) Check his pulse. I'll listen for a heart-beat.
C	(To A) Do you know any First Aid?
A	Huh…
C	Can you give the kiss of life?
A	No. I don't think so.
B	I can't hear anything.
C	There's a slight pulse. I think I can feel something.
B	(Listening closely to D's chest) I can hear beating. It's very quiet.
A	Is he going to be alright?

Pause. B and C help D to sit up.

C   Are you OK?

B   I thought you were a goner then.

C   Thank God.

D   (Very faintly) What happened? Where am I?

C   It's O.K. Don't worry. We'll get you home. (To A) Give me a hand with him.

C and A help D to stand.

B   Here's the bus.

A   Shouldn't we try to get an ambulance?

D   (Faintly) No. I want to go home.

A   You must go to hospital. I'll go up to the 'phone box and call an ambulance.

C   He said he doesn't want to go to hospital.

A   But that's ridiculous. He needs to be checked to see if he's alright.

B   Here comes the bus. Let's help him get on.

A   He needs help. Medical help! This isn't right.

B   Are you going to help us get him on?

C puts a hand out for the bus.

D	I feel a bit better now. I think I can stand on my own.
B	(To D) Are you sure?
D	I don't want to be any trouble.
B	It's no trouble at all. We'll see you home safely. We'll all stay with you until your stop then we'll take you home.
A	(To D) Is there anyone at home?
D	No. Only the cat.
C	Come on. It's nearly here.
A	You need someone to stay with you in case you have another attack.
D	Attack?
A	Your heart.
D	My heart? What do you mean?
B	What are you talking about?
C	Are you lot getting on this bus or not?
A	I don't understand. I thought you were....
C	If you don't stop chattering you'll miss it.

They all board the bus